# DEDICATION

This book is first dedicated to The Great Shepherd, our Lord Jesus Christ, Who has counted me faithful, putting me into the ministry among His Sheepfold. It is dedicated secondly to all the undershepherds who have taken His yoke upon themselves to lay down their lives for the sheep. It is my solemn prayer that many leaders will be helped in their God-given responsibilities by all who may read this book, and that those children of God who have been separated from the fellowship of the local church will be restored and refreshed.

*Well done, good and faithful servant.*

ഇ Matthew 25:23 ര

# Take My Yoke Upon You

## Fulfilling Your THREE-DIMENSIONAL DESTINY in Christ

EBED
PUBLICATIONS
*In love, serve one another*

by

Dr. John Polis

**Take My Yoke Upon You**



All Scripture references are from the Authorized King James Version of the Bible, unless otherwise noted. References marked **NIV** are from the New International Version of the Bible, © copyright 1973, 1978, 1984 by International Bible Society, Colorado Springs, Colorado. References marked **AMPLIFIED** are from the Amplified Bible, © copyright 1987 by the Zondervan Corporation and the Lockman Foundation, La Habra Foundation, California.

EBED Publications is a division of McDougal Publishing, Hagerstown, Maryland.

Published by:

EBED Publications
P.O. Box 3595
Hagerstown, MD 21742-3595

ISBN 1-884369-53-7

Printed in the United States of America

# Introduction

*But he that knew not, and did commit things worthy of stripes, shall be beaten with few stripes. For unto whomsoever much is given, of him shall be much required: and to whom men have committed much, of him they will ask the more.*

Luke 12:48

Every believer has a God-given destiny, and this is no small gift. It is a treasure to be evaluated and protected.

Many have never thought of destiny as something that requires their faithful stewardship, have never considered that destiny is a God-given responsibility. Therefore, in the following pages, I hope to reveal destiny in a new light and to cause the reader to discover the three-dimensional application of destiny to the Christian walk. Fulfilling our destiny is fulfilling our God-given responsibility.

The first dimension of study will be the relationship between the believer and the Body of Christ. We will examine destiny's purpose in that relationship and our responsibility in the fulfillment of The Great Commission.

The second dimension of study will be the relationship of the believer to the local church. Because of its importance to our spiritual and physical well-being, I have dedicated the greater part of this work to the study of this dimension, and in the examination of this aspect of destiny, I will show the reader the path to greater fulfillment in Christ.

The third and final dimension of our destiny will be seen as our personal relationship to destiny. What talents has God given you personally? Will you, as a believer, put these talents to work for your Lord? Or will you find a convenient place to bury them? Christ has given each of us *"much"* and He requires *"much"* of us.

As you are able to discover your three-dimensional destiny in Christ, and begin to apply the responsibility of destiny to your own life, you will find freedom and release. You will also find new peace and joy.

To some, talk about taking on yokes of responsibility may sound intimidating, but I trust that as the pages of this book flip through your fingers, you will be challenged and will see that it is wise and desirable to take on the Savior's yoke. After all, He said that His yoke was *"easy."*

*Dr. John Polis*
*Fairmont, West Virginia*

# Part I:

# *Your Destiny in Christ*

# Table of Contents

*For the kingdom of heaven is as a man travelling into a far country, who called his own servants, and delivered unto them his goods. And unto one he gave five talents, to another two, and to another one; to every man according to his several ability; ... .*

*After a long time the lord of those servants cometh, and reckoneth with them. ... He that had received five talents came and brought other five talents, saying, Lord, thou deliveredst unto me five talents: behold, I have gained beside them five talents more. His lord said unto him, Well done, thou good and faithful servant: thou hast been faithful over a few things, I will make thee ruler over many things: enter thou into the joy of thy lord. ... Then he which had received the one talent came and said, Lord, I knew thee that thou art an hard man, ... and I was afraid, and went and hid thy talent in the earth: lo, there thou hast that is thine.*

*His lord answered and said unto him, Thou wicked and slothful servant, ... thou oughtest therefore to have put my money to the exchangers ... . Take therefore the talent ... and give it unto him which hath ten talents. For unto every one that hath shall be given, and he shall have abundance: but from him that hath not shall be taken away even that which he hath.*

Matthew 25:14-30

# Foreword by Dr. Don Meares

I first met Dr. John Polis several years ago when he, along with many other pastors, became involved in an organization devoted to strengthening the local church and its leaders. Over the last few years, he and I have sat together for hours at council meetings — strategizing, planning, defining and refining goals. We have shared serious times, as well as times of fellowship and laughter. If we have one thing in common, it is this: we love the local church and its leaders, and we desire to see them strengthened in every way.

My colleague John Polis is a man of God whose life and ministry touch many pastors and church leaders. His experiences — as husband, father, church planter, pastor and spiritual leader of fifteen years — qualify him to speak biblical truths with deep insight.

I was particularly intrigued by Dr. Polis' choice of a title. It was Jesus who said, *"Take my yoke upon you."* John had told me that his book had to do with individual and corporate destiny and because these are topics on which I often speak and on which I have written, I was keenly interested in hearing his perspective, which I found to be indeed unique.

I appreciate the fact that Dr. Polis has taken a difficult subject, one which can easily be over-spiritualized, and has brought it down to a level of the personal responsibility of the individual believer. I concur wholeheartedly with his challenge to believers, to become planted in a local assembly, to learn the vision of the leadership and, with meekness and lowliness of heart, to take that particular yoke upon themselves. This is godly advice which will guide the believer into a practical participation of divine destiny.

*Take My Yoke Upon You* is an inspiring and motivating book, filled with sound scriptural advice and pearls of wisdom. It is clear, focused and discerning. I feel certain that any person who reads and embraces the truth within it will benefit tremendously. I have read many books which are aimed at motivating Christians to fulfill their destiny in Christ, and I can say without hesitation that *Take My Yoke Upon You* is one of the best.

*Dr. Don Meares*
*Upper Marlboro, Maryland*

## CHAPTER ONE

# DISCOVERING YOUR DESTINY

*After a long time the lord of those servants cometh, and reckoneth with them. And so he that had received five talents came and brought other five talents, saying, Lord, thou deliveredst unto me five talents: behold, I have gained beside them five talents more. His lord said unto him, Well done, thou good and faithful servant: thou hast been faithful over a few things, I will make thee ruler over many things: ENTER THOU INTO THE JOY OF THY LORD.*

Matthew 25:19-21

What is destiny? Christians often think of it as having to do with the future. Sometimes they think of it as a vision that God has for their life, or the fulfillment of prophecies that speak of a job that He would have them accomplish in due time.

This may be the meaning of destiny in its "ultimate sense," but this "ultimate sense" is only one slice of the pie. Destiny is also related to "today" — the here and now, and in this sense, means responsibility, today's responsibility.

Solomon, the preacher, wrote:

> *Whatsoever thy hand finds to do, DO IT with all thy might.* Ecclesiastes 9:10

Before reaching destiny's ultimate goal, before the clock's hands reach midnight, so to speak, there are myriad deeds to which we must dedicate our hands. It is time to put our hands to the labor, for destiny is fulfilled today, not just in the future.

Jesus taught this concept of destiny in His parables:

> *His lord said unto him, Well done, GOOD AND FAITHFUL servant; thou hast been faithful over a few things, I will make thee ruler over many things: enter thou into the joy of thy lord.*
> Matthew 25:23

Before this servant could avail himself of *"the joy"* his lord had prepared for him, he had to be found *"good and faithful ... over a few things."* He had to fulfill his present destiny. So, in this parable, Jesus was teaching responsibility.

The most intriguing thing about this verse is the

reward the Lord offers to those who are faithful in fulfilling their God-given responsibility — more responsibility. Some will become rulers over five cities and some over ten cities, and all because they have been faithful with their present God-given responsibilities. So destiny begins today.

If you can come to understand your God-given responsibilities, therefore, you will understand an important aspect of your destiny. If you can begin now to get to where you are ultimately going, you will be successful and will experience great fulfillment in life. So fulfilling any God-given responsibility, no matter how small or insignificant, is an important step in fulfilling your divine destiny.

Teaching abounds in the Word of God on the theme of responsibility. Having established the connection between destiny and responsibility, therefore, let us now take a look at one such portion of Scripture:

> *And we desire that every one of you do show the same diligence to the full assurance of hope unto the end; that ye BE NOT SLOTHFUL, but followers of them who through faith and patience inherit* [or possess] *the promises.*
>
> Hebrews 6:11-12

*Diligence* (responsibility), *not slothful, full of faith and patience* — these characteristics demonstrate maturity.

Those of us who are parents will often observe changing traits in our children's lives, as they grow through childhood to puberty, then from adolescence to adulthood. Once they begin to accept responsibility for their own lives, we acknowledge that they are maturing.

I believe that God looks at our lives in the same way. As our Heavenly Father, He watches us grow spiritually. In the beginning, He frequently sees others take more spiritual responsibility for our lives than we do ourselves. Other mature Christians carry us spiritually — praying for us, and feeding us the Word of God. If we stumble, they are there to pick us up. At some point, it is the Father's good pleasure for us to take charge of our own spiritual wellbeing. The writer of Hebrews, therefore, asserted that when a believer takes responsibility for answers to his or her own prayers, he or she is showing maturity. And that is pleasing to God. What a wonderful day it is when a person begins to accept responsibility for getting his own prayers answered!

The Scripture say: *"We desire that every one of you"* — not just a few people, but *every one of you* — obtain answers to your prayers and possess the promises of God through faith and patience. But don't forget to work at being diligent, to work at being personally responsible. While waiting on God to see the appropriation of His promised blessings in answer to prayer, apply faith and exercise patience. This is God's way.

Once we have learned to pray for ourselves and get answers from God, we will have reached a new level of maturity.

God is a rewarder of them that diligently seek Him. Let us examine what His Word has to say to us in this regard:

> *But without faith it is impossible to please God, for he that cometh to God must believe that He is and that He is a rewarder of them that DILIGENTLY SEEK Him.* Hebrews 11:6

Diligence! Responsibility! These themes are echoed throughout the Scriptures and just won't go away. God rewards responsible and mature believers. Commit yourself to seeking God, and the Bible says that you will be rewarded. Not only must we take responsibility for answered prayer, but we are responsible for seeking God and coming into our full stature in Christ.

Personal productivity, being fruitful, is another area that reflects maturity. The grocery store gives us an easy example of the relationship between productivity and fruitfulness. If you enter such a store to buy some produce, you go to the fruit department or the vegetable department, depending on what you are looking for. Jesus fixed fruitfulness (productivity) as a target for His followers:

*Herein is my Father glorified that ye BEAR MUCH FRUIT; so shall ye be my disciples.*
John 15:8

Spiritual productivity, reproducing ourselves in others, means taking responsibility for what we've learned. It means not needing to be taught repeatedly, over and over again, the first principles of the doctrines of Christ. It means being able to teach others:

*For when for the time ye ought to be teachers, ye have need that one teach you again which be the first principles of the oracles of God; and are become such as have need of milk, and not of strong meat. For every one that useth milk is unskillful in the word of righteousness: for he is a babe. But STRONG MEAT BELONGETH TO THEM THAT ARE OF FULL AGE, even those who by reason of use have their senses exercised to discern both good and evil.* Hebrews 5:12-14

We must grow up so that we can tackle life's more challenging tasks.

Timothy had a big job. As a young man, he had been given charge of a large church in Ephesus, a church with some serious problems.

The Apostle Paul, Timothy's spiritual father, wrote to his son, encouraging him in the faith. His advice to the young man was to find some faithful men, men who would act responsibly when they had been entrusted with something:

> *And the things that thou has heard of me among many witnesses, the same COMMIT THOU TO FAITHFUL MEN, who shall be able to teach others also.* 2 Timothy 2:2

Timothy should search for some mature and willing men, men desirous of personal productivity and ready to teach to others what they had learned themselves. That's good advice.

Jesus advised us to be responsible people:

> *But he that knew not, and did commit things worthy of stripes, shall be beaten with few stripes. For unto whomsoever MUCH IS GIVEN, OF HIM SHALL BE MUCH REQUIRED: and to whom men have committed much, of him they will ask the more.* Luke 12:48

Solomon observed:

> *He becometh poor that dealeth with a slack hand; but the hand of the DILIGENT maketh rich.*
> Proverbs 10:4

Productivity is the result of diligence and maturity and a failure to take such responsibility leads to poverty, both spiritual and physical, and God's displeasure. We must each take responsibility for our own spiritual progress and development:

> *Wherefore let him that thinketh he standeth TAKE HEED lest he fall.* 1 Corinthians 10:4

Maintaining a consistent walk of faith before God, watching, to avoid stumbling, is a believer's individual duty:

> *EXAMINE YOURSELVES, whether ye be in the faith; PROVE YOUR OWN SELVES. Know ye not your own selves, how that Jesus Christ is in you, except ye be reprobates.*
>
> 2 Corinthians 13:5

Since church leaders will oversee the spiritual well-being of others, they must be responsible people. The Greek word translated as *elder* is *"presbuterion"* and means, *one who is not a novice in the faith, but a mature believer*. We need more true *elders* in all of our churches.

When Paul was leaving Ephesus, he gathered the elders of the church together and told them:

> *TAKE HEED therefore unto yourselves, and to all the flock, over the which the Holy Ghost hath*

*made you overseers, to feed the church of God, which He hath purchased with His own blood.*
Acts 20:28

He was calling them to account for their God-given responsibilities. They would be responsible for the flock, *"the church of God,"* but they would first be responsible for their own spiritual welfare. And that makes sense. You can't manage someone else's life until you can first manage your own. You can't help another person with their affairs if your affairs are in disarray. So Paul said to these church leaders, *"Take heed ... to yourself."* Get yourself squared away. See that *you* are under control yourself. See that *you* do not give place to the devil. See that *you* walk by faith and not by sight. See that *you* walk in love. See that *you* keep yourself unspotted by the world. Then you will be able to oversee the flock of God and help others to do what you have been able to accomplish. That is your responsibility in the Holy Ghost. Responsibility is a measure of maturity.

An important part of discovering personal destiny, then, is finding out what your God-given daily responsibilities are and fulfilling them. You should start today:

*Whatsoever thy hand findeth to do, DO IT with all thy might;* Ecclesiastes 9:10

If you are carrying out God-given responsibility,

you are fulfilling personal destiny. I have known far too many Christians who were like the old saying: "So heavenly minded they were no earthly good." These people seem to live so much in the future they can't get anything done in the present. They're constantly looking to see what their lives will be someday. They always have their mind centered on the future. Sometime in the vague future they will have more time to do the things they know they should do. Sometime in the vague future they will have good health that will allow them to accomplish their goals. Maybe when the kids are grown and gone from the home, they can achieve their destiny, maybe. People like this sit unproductive for months at a time or even years, waiting for the day of their ultimate destiny. What they don't realize is that their ultimate destiny is reached one day at a time.

God gives us greater responsibilities when He finds us to be faithful with smaller ones:

> *He that is faithful in that which is least is faithful ALSO IN MUCH: and he that is unjust in the least is unjust also in much.* Luke 16:10

When we have been faithful over some small matter, God can then entrust us with greater responsibility. This means that a believer cannot start out as a leader of a local church. A new believer cannot be a pastor, a teacher, a prophet, or an apostle. Most cannot quickly become a deacon or even an usher.

Each must begin with a lesser responsibility, but if we are faithful, God will quickly increase our responsibilities.

Many desire promotion, but they have no idea what it's really all about. Promotion in spiritual things means being given greater spiritual responsibility by God. It is not a position. It is a privilege to serve.

Many people equate position with promotion, and there may be some truth to that concept, but promotion's most important aspect is the taking on of greater responsibility. This is God's reward for faithfulness and proven character.

Paul wrote:

> *But I trust in the Lord Jesus to send Timotheus shortly unto you, that I also may be of good comfort, when I know your state. For I have no man like-minded, who will naturally care for your state. For all seek their own, not the things which are Jesus Christ's. But ye know the proof of him, that, as a son with the father,* HE HATH SERVED WITH ME IN THE GOSPEL. *Him therefore I hope to send presently, so soon as I shall see how it will go with me. But I trust in the Lord that I also myself shall come shortly.*
>
> Philippians 2:19-24

Timothy was privileged to be Paul's number two

man. What an honor! Timothy actually took Paul's place on some special assignments. But Timothy was given such responsibility because his character had been proven during years of service.

Individually, we accept responsibilities on various levels. If you are single, you have a responsibility to your parents. If you are married, you are responsible to your mate. And if you are a parent, you must embrace the responsibility of raising your children.

In relationship to the Work of God on Earth, there are three levels, or dimensions, of responsibility, and in the following chapter we will deal with each of them. Understanding this three-dimensional aspect of destiny and its relationship to responsibility will help us to accept and fulfill God's ultimate plan for us — one day at a time.

Destiny has two aspects: the present and the future, the daily and the ultimate. Has God given you a personal prophetic vision? Then He has also given you daily responsibilities that stand between you and your future. Always remember Jesus' teachings about the *talents.* What have you done with the talents He gave you? What you do with them today is as much a part of your destiny as hearing the Lord say one day in the future, *enter into the joy of thy Lord.* The task is at hand. Let's get started.

# Part II:

# *The First Dimension of Your Destiny*

## Chapter Two

# Your Participation In the Body of Christ

*Come unto me, all ye that labour and are heavy laden, and I will give you rest. TAKE MY YOKE UPON YOU, and learn of me; for I am meek and lowly in heart: and ye shall find rest unto your souls. For MY YOKE IS EASY, and my burden is light.*

Matthew 11:28-30

You are probably already a member of the Body of Christ or you wouldn't be reading this book. Let me congratulate you. You have joined a wonderful entity. The Body of Christ is a wonderful thing. By being part of Christ, we lose the inherent sense of human limitations and boundaries. The Body of Christ is universal and unlimited:

*For by one Spirit are we all baptized into ONE*

*BODY, whether we be Jews or Gentiles, whether we be bond or free; and have been all made to drink into ONE SPIRIT.* 1 Corinthians 12:13

Each born-again Christian must embrace this new "Body" identity. We should know, deep inside, that we are a part of the Church of the Lord Jesus Christ — His Body. This is the first level of responsibility, or the first dimension of destiny; a starting place for Christian maturity and growth.

Every believer is a member of Christ's universal, corporate Body. Every believer has a universal or corporate destiny. I like to call this: "corporate destiny in the universal sense." Simply, it means that we are a part of the Body of Christ, the Universal Church of the Lord Jesus Christ.

The word "corporate" refers to a "body." Because I am part of the corporate Body of Christ, I have a destiny, a correlation, to the Universal Church of the Lord Jesus Christ. Praise God for that!

Jesus left His disciples with a great commandment which we have come to call The Great Commission:

*And he said unto them, GO YE INTO ALL THE WORLD, and preach the gospel to every creature. He that believeth and is baptized shall be saved; but he that believeth not shall be damned. And these signs shall follow them that believe; In my name shall they cast out devils; they shall speak with new tongues; They shall take up serpents; and if they drink any deadly thing, it shall not hurt them; they shall lay hands on the sick, and they shall recover. So then after the Lord had spoken unto them, he was received up into heaven, and sat on the right hand of God. And they went forth, and preached every where, the Lord working with them, and confirming the word with signs following. Amen.* Mark 16:15-20

Jesus gave His Body a destiny, a great responsibility, The Great Commission. This is the responsibility of the whole church — worldwide. If you consider yourself a member of the "whole church," then Christ's Commission is also a personal commission. "Worldwide" includes you and me — individually, so The Great Commission is a personal responsibility. With the help of the Holy Spirit, we are to be soul winners and disciple makers. We should readily accept that identity and that responsibility.

In his letter to the Colossians, Paul established the fact that Jesus Christ is the Head of the Church:

*And HE IS THE HEAD OF THE BODY, the church: who is the beginning, the firstborn from the dead; that in all things he might have the preeminence.* Colossians 1:18

To the Ephesians, he wrote:

> *And hath put all things under his feet, and GAVE HIM TO BE THE HEAD over all things to the church, which is his body, the fulness of him that filleth all in all.* Ephesians 1:22-23

Jesus Christ is the Head — the ultimate authority — over the entire Body of Christ. He is our Lord and Master. He said:

> *Come unto me, all ye that labour and are heavy laden, and I will give you rest. TAKE MY YOKE UPON YOU, AND LEARN OF ME; for I am meek and lowly in heart: and ye shall find rest unto your souls. For my yoke is easy, and my burden is light.* Matthew 11:28-30

A *yoke,* in this case, represents responsibility. Jesus was saying, "Take My responsibilities as your own responsibilities. Doing this, learn from Me. I'm meek and lowly of heart, so it won't be too hard for you."

Christ's yoke, His responsibility, His destiny is part of a learning and maturing experience, a personal training ground for each individual. It is also a Body experience, for He said *"come ... all."* His invitation is for the entire Body. The question then is: What is my part in all of this? Where do I fit in?

You and I, as individual members of the Body of

Christ, must find our individual part in The Great Commission and make an effort to get involved. Part of accepting the yoke of the Lord is coming to understand what He means for us as individuals to be doing and finding our individual place in the worldwide harvest.

Jesus' personal imperative from the Father was to reconcile the world to God:

> *To wit, that God was in Christ, RECONCILING THE WORLD UNTO HIMSELF, not imputing their trespasses unto them; and hath committed unto us the word of reconciliation. Now then we are ambassadors for Christ, as though God did beseech you by us: we pray you in Christ's stead, be ye reconciled to God. For He hath made Him to be sin for us, who knew no sin; that we might be made the righteousness of God in Him.*
>
> 2 Corinthians 5:19-21

This task was not only for Jesus. He did what only He could do, then He passed the torch to us in the form of The Great Commission. Paul wrote to the Corinthians that it was also their job to get the word of reconciliation out. They were to be ambassadors for Christ, His representatives in the Earth.

Repeatedly, in the Acts of the Apostles, the members of the early church took the yoke of Jesus Christ upon themselves. They continued the work Jesus had begun. They understood His yoke, and they understood that their personal destiny was fulfilled in being ambassadors of reconciliation. They counted it a privilege to be sent by God to lost sinners everywhere.

No matter what church group you may be part of, and no matter what name hangs above its door, if you are born again, you are a part of the Body of Christ. The members of His Body share one yoke: fulfilling The Great Commission and reconciling the world to Christ. He said:

> *GO YE THEREFORE, and teach all nations, baptizing them in the Name of the Father, and of the Son, and of the Holy Ghost: teaching them to observe all things whatsoever I have commanded you: and lo, I am with you alway, even unto the end of the world.* Matthew 28:19-20

The Great Commission has several different parts. Preaching the Gospel is one aspect. Teaching the Word of God is another. Then there's casting out devils, healing the sick, speaking with new tongues, and exercising dominion over all the power of the enemy. Have you become a Great-Commission Christian? Have you found your corporate destiny in the universal sense? Can you say right now, "I have taken Christ's yoke upon me and accepted responsibility in fulfilling The Great Commission. I have made that my personal responsibility." Until you can declare that The Great Commission has become a personal matter, you haven't taken Christ's yoke upon you and you are not yet fulfilling your destiny in Him.

Have you felt the satisfaction of fulfilling God-given responsibility by leading someone to Christ? If you have, you know that leading another person to Christ releases great joy, both in Heaven and on Earth. It is because God's will is being done in Earth as it is in Heaven.

When a sinner is born again, Heaven erupts with sounds of gladness, and the individual believers, both the person who has been saved and the person who has led that soul to the feet of Jesus, feel that overflow of rejoicing and explode with the joy of the Lord. The new believer is feeling the joy of being part of God's Kingdom, that Kingdom which is *righteousness, peace and joy in the Holy Ghost.*

Which of the two believers is feeling the most joy: the one who has been newly born again or the one who led him or her to Christ? While it is an exciting time for anyone coming into the Kingdom for the first time, we must say that a far greater personal fulfillment comes to the Christian who carries out His God-given responsibility.

What a wonderful moment! Heaven is rejoicing, the new believer is rejoicing, the faithful servant is rejoicing and Hell is trembling because it is losing another battle.

Jesus illustrated His yoke for us by using the servant's towel to wash the disciple's feet at the Passover meal:

> *Jesus knowing that the Father had given all things into his hands, and that he was come from God, and went to God; He riseth from supper, and laid aside his garments; and* TOOK A TOWEL, AND GIRDED HIMSELF. *After that he poureth water into a bason, and began to wash the disciples' feet, and to wipe them with the towel wherewith he was girded. Then cometh he to Simon Peter: and Peter saith unto him, Lord, dost thou wash my feet? Jesus answered and said unto him, What I do thou knowest not now; but thou shalt know hereafter. Peter saith unto him, Thou shalt never wash my feet. Jesus answered him, If I wash thee not, thou hast no part with me.*
>
> John 13:3-8

By bowing to serve others, He showed us that serving God means serving people. He thus set an example, not only for His immediate disciples but for all who would choose to serve Him in the centuries ahead.

In order to take up the servant's towel, you must be humble or broken. The proud and haughty will never gird themselves with the towel of service.

It is revealing to note what was going through Jesus' mind as He performed this humble act. "... *knowing that the Father had given all things into his hands, and that he was come from God, and went to God; He ... laid aside his garments; and took a towel.*" If ever there lived One who had the right to be proud it was Jesus. After all, these were simple fishermen and He was the King of kings. Yet, He did not refuse the towel of service.

Surely, Jesus didn't have to do that. Wasn't it enough to teach and to heal the sick? Why did He have to wash someone's stinky feet?

This is exactly the problem we face when trying to get the average Christian to understand the basics of service to God. They want to serve God, Whom they know to be totally good, but they are not so sure about serving one another, because they know each other's flaws. They find it difficult, therefore, to accept the towel of the servant.

Jesus said to Peter (and I paraphrase), "Unless you become like Me, you have no part in Me. Allow Me to wash your feet — leaving you an example that you should serve each other." If we are not willing to do what He was willing to do, we cannot be His disciples and we cannot claim a place in His harvest today.

If you want to be part of what God is doing in these days, if you want to be part of His move, part of His anointing that is being poured out, you must become like the Master, clothed with humility, clad with the garment of service.

Peter, in his office of apostle, wrote to the believers at Rome:

> *Likewise, ye younger, submit yourselves unto the elder. Yea, all of you be subject one to another, and be CLOTHED with humility: for God resisteth the proud, and giveth grace to the humble.*
>
> 1 Peter 5:5

Just as Jesus *girded* Himself with the servant's towel, we must be *CLOTHED with humility.* What Jesus did, and what we are enjoined to do, are one and the same – take the yoke of the Father upon us.

While Jesus was washing his feet, Peter obviously learned a great lesson, a lesson that he later taught to others: clothe yourself with the spirit of the servant.

It is always easy to recognize a person who has clothed himself or herself with humility, for he or she has a servant's heart.

When we learn to serve others in the Body of Christ we begin to carry out our corporate destiny in the universal sense. This is an important first step because without a servant's heart, we will be frustrated when trying to function in any of destiny's dimensions.

## Your Participation In the Body of Christ

Paul reminded the Philippians:

> *Let this mind be in you, which was also in Christ Jesus: Who, being in the form of God, thought it not robbery to be equal with God: But made himself of no reputation, and took upon him the form of a servant, and was made in the likeness of men: And being found in fashion as a man, he humbled himself, and became obedient unto death, even the death of the cross. Wherefore God also hath highly exalted him, and given him a name which is above every name: That at the name of Jesus every knee should bow, of things in heaven, and things in earth, and things under the earth; And that every tongue should confess that Jesus Christ is Lord, to the glory of God the Father.*
>
> Philippians 2:5-11

This is our corporate destiny in the universal sense. With the heart of a true servant, we are to accept personal responsibility for our part in fulfilling The Great Commission. This is not an option. We cannot pick and choose what we will do in the Kingdom. Every responsibility must be carried out faithfully.

Knowing this, Paul wrote:

> *Who now rejoice in my sufferings for you, and fill up that which is behind of the afflictions of*

### *Take My Yoke Upon You*

*Christ in my flesh for His Body's sake, which is the Church.* Colossians 1:24

The Apostle Paul was so identified with Christ's yoke that he was willing to suffer whatever was necessary to see that the objectives put forth by his Lord were reached. Therefore, he allowed himself to be broken, wounded, beaten and battered. He shed many tears for the sake of the Gospel, but he did it willingly. He was ready to go all the way for Jesus, having chosen to clothe himself in the servant's garb.

This is the first dimension of your destiny, and I trust that you are ready to continue.

# Part III:

# *The Second Dimension of Your Destiny*

## Chapter Three

# The Principle of Faithfulness

*And if ye have not been faithful in that which is ANOTHER MAN'S, who shall give you that which is your own?*

Luke 16:12

A key principle in God's Kingdom is faithfulness. Before something is entrusted to us, Jesus said, we must be faithful with that which has been entrusted to someone else.

God calls those He wants to place in leadership over His Body. He never looks their way, however, in the sense of giving them their own ministry, until He sees that they are faithfully joined to the ministry of others. So, although God does the choosing, much depends on you and me.

In fact, each individual is accountable before God to learn what his personal responsibilities are. And until he knows and is able to exercise that responsibility, his job is to share in his pastor's yoke. When we are willing to share in the yoke (and thus the destiny), of the leadership set over us, we set ourselves into a new place of possibility and potential in God's Kingdom. I like to call this our "corporate destiny in the local sense."

Many Christians don't understand this dimension of destiny. They readily agree that they should take on a Great-Commission commitment, identifying themselves with the whole Body of Christ, the Universal Church. But when it comes to the local assembly, they wash their hands. The thought of submitting themselves to the leadership of "some man," as they say, is repugnant. These people are so "spiritual" that finding their yoke in the local body under a local leader is beneath them. They only answer to God.

There are many transient Christians within the Body of Christ. I call them "professional visitors." Someone has said that this kind of believer belongs to "the seven churches." They come to church one Sunday and say, "I am visiting today." They come back the next Sunday, and they are still visiting. After six months, they're still visiting. Then suddenly they find another church to "visit." This goes on and on, and on. These are not stable Christians. They are only "professional visitors."

If a believer wants to do something for God, and is seeking greater responsibility in the Kingdom, it is their duty to settle down somewhere and get behind a man of God. They must find their place in the local church and get busy. If all of the "professional visitors" could just get a vision and see that submission to a local church is the answer to fulfilling personal destiny, it would change our churches.

I believe that every one of us needs to get "yoked up," hooked up to the load, and find his or her place within the Body of Christ. We must understand that we have been born into the family of God for a purpose and placed within the Body of Christ by the divine action of the Holy Ghost.

For some reason, getting placed in a local body of believers is difficult for many. If we accept that we are part of the Body of Christ through the new birth, we have no choice. This is God's will for us. He places us as He chooses:

> *God hath set some in the church, first apostles, secondarily prophets, thirdly teachers, after that miracles, then gifts of healings, helps, governments, diversities of tongues.*
>
> 1 Corinthians 12:28

The Word of God tells us that He establishes ministry gifts in the Church, both in the Universal Church and in the local church. So God has a local church for you, a local body to set you into, where you can identify with His people. He wants to connect you to a spiritual family:

> *God setteth the solitary in families: He bringeth out those which are bound with chains: but the rebellious dwell in a dry land.* Psalm 68:6

Unfortunately, this step into destiny's second dimension requires a level of commitment that many Christians are unwilling to make nowadays. They are willing to identify with the Body of Christ universally (at least in word, though perhaps not in deed), and recognize Jesus Christ as Head of the Church, but they won't recognize the man (the pastor) that Jesus has placed as head in the local church. In so doing, they destine themselves to a life of immaturity.

After Jesus rose from the dead, He said to His disciples:

> *And, behold, I send the promise of my Father upon you: but tarry ye in the city of Jerusalem, until ye be endued with power from on high.*
>
> Luke 24:49

He specifically told them where they were to wait for His move in their lives, and He still tells individual Christians where to find their Jerusalem, where to go to church and participate in the local body. The problem is: are they willing to listen?

One of the strongest New Testament declarations concerning our need for loyalty to a local assembly is found in the letter to the Hebrews:

> *Let us hold fast the profession of our faith without wavering; (for he is faithful that promised;) And let us consider one another to provoke unto love and to good works: NOT FORSAKING THE ASSEMBLING OF OURSELVES TOGETHER, as the manner of some is; but exhorting one another: and so much the more, as ye see the day approaching.* Hebrews 10:23-25

Nothing could be more clear.

Day by day, with greater intensity, the Holy Spirit is drawing believers into local congregations, to assemble themselves with those of like precious faith, but He also points out in this message to the Hebrews the manner of conduct of some. It is to disassociate themselves from the rest of the Body. He urges us to do the opposite, more since we see the day of Christ's return approaching. We must insist on sticking close to the assembly, sticking close to the corporate Body of Christ.

I am encouraged to see it happening. Local churches all over the country and, indeed, all over the world, which are moving in true New Testament faith, are exploding. Believers who have been scattered as sheep without a shepherd are being drawn by the Great Shepherd into local congregations to be nurtured. These are places where God has put His Name and established His ministry under chosen leaders to whom He has given the oversight.

Because of this, we are seeing a time of unparalleled church growth.

Many countries now have congregations that range from twenty-five to a hundred thousand members. It is because the Lord is coming soon and He is moving mightily just before His coming. He is assembling the family of God, calling us forth to a solemn time of gathering together. It is for equipping, for training, and for preparation for these last days.

It won't be long now that you will see the Lord coming in the air and hear His voice, saying, "Come up hither." In that moment, His Church, His glorious Bride, without spot and without blemish, prepared as a bride for her bridegroom, will be received by Him into glory. How beautiful she will be in that moment!

The spots and wrinkles that will be nowhere to be found in that day represent the character flaws that we all presently have. Thank God that He is ironing them out:

The Scriptures declare:

> *Let the Word of Christ dwell in you richly in all wisdom; TEACHING AND ADMONISHING one another in psalms and hymns and spiritual songs, singing with grace in your hearts to the Lord.* Colossians 3:16

It is possible that the Lord will have to do some

ironing on some of us at the last minute, but Paul's description of the preparation process, *teaching and admonishing,* sounds a lot like what we do daily and weekly in the local assembly. That may be why we always have problems in local churches. We are just getting everything ironed out of us.

We are to help each other, working together in relationship, ironing out our character defects. Until someone is unkind to us, we can't practice being kind. When other people's character weaknesses rub against our own, it produces friction, and things can get hot. That helps us develop the fruit of the Spirit. Jesus said:

> *But I say unto you which hear, Love your enemies, do good to them which hate you, Bless them that curse you, and pray for them which despitefully use you.* Luke 6:27-28

We reach the pinnacle of our Christian maturity through the difficulties we encounter in relationships with carnal people. That includes even the unsaved and those possessed of demons. Our best shines through in the most difficult situations, and that is the glory of the Christian life. Through suffering, character is developed in us.

Paul taught the Roman Christians that suffering produces endurance, endurance produces proven character, and proven character produces hope —

the confident expectancy of good to come to pass in our lives (Romans 5:1-5). So the end result, the product of the trials that we face and the difficult encounters we experience, is the godly character that is formed within us. Absolutely everything works to our good.

As the Day of the Lord approaches, God is gathering His people together in local churches so that their character can be developed, so that Christ-likeness can be formed within them, so that they can become vessels of honor, sanctified and meet for the Master's use.

Recently, God revealed to me a beautiful truth in the following passage:

> *But in a great house there are not only vessels of GOLD AND OF SILVER, but also of WOOD AND OF EARTH; and some to honour, and some to dishonour. If a man therefore purge himself from these, he shall be a vessel unto honour, sanctified, and meet for the master's use, and prepared unto every good work. Flee also youthful lusts: but follow righteousness, faith, charity, peace, with them that call on the Lord out of a pure heart. But foolish and unlearned questions avoid, knowing that they do gender strifes. And the servant of the Lord must not strive; but be gentle unto all men, apt to teach, patient.* 2 Timothy 2:20-24

In every great house there are not only vessels of

wood and clay, but there are some of gold and silver, some to honor and some to dishonor. God showed me that for many years, as a pastor, I had tried to polish wood and clay, and all that I got was splinters in my hands. He showed me that before a vessel can be polished, its nature has to change. It must be transformed from wood and clay to silver and gold.

In this passage written to Timothy, God is speaking about Christian people and saying that they are vessels in His house. Every born-again Christian is a vessel for God's glory. Paul wrote:

> *We have this treasure in earthen vessels.*
>
> 2 Corinthians 4:7

Some may be vessels of wood, or vessels of clay, and to become vessels of silver and gold, they need a fundamental changed in their nature. Only then can they be polished and refined. Only then can the image of Jesus Christ shine forth from them.

How are our natures to be changed into more malleable materials? Through brokenness and contrition of spirit, through deliverance from stubbornness and self-will (rebellion, the tendency to resist God's plan for our lives). We must be broken until we cry out for deliverance. We must ask Him to eliminate our self-motivation and transform us into vessels of silver or of gold. When that happens our value will be multiplied many times over. Items made from silver and gold far outlast the usefulness of items made from wood and clay. Then, once we are broken, once we are transformed from wood and clay to silver and gold, the polishing process can begin.

I find such a release in this truth because it lets me know that I don't have to polish wood and clay. I don't have to polish stubborn and rebellious people, those that are unwilling to be a part of God's program. As a pastor, I am not responsible to try to bring such lives into perfection. My only obligation towards them is to pray that they will be broken, to pray that their wills would be surrendered to God, to pray that their selfish agendas will be destroyed by the Holy Ghost, and to keep praying until they seek to do the will of God with a servant's heart.

When I see the servant's heart, that tells me that we are making progress. A servant's heart is the sign of a vessel which is made of silver or gold, not just a heart of service toward God, whom we can't see, but service to people, whom we can see. So I identify those who have been changed from wood and clay to silver and gold by their servant's heart.

Paul wrote to Timothy:

> *And the servant of the Lord must not strive; but be gentle unto all men, apt to teach, patient.*
>
> 2 Timothy 2:24

How is a servant's heart revealed? It is through relationship with other members of the Body of Christ. The role of a servant cannot be assumed without someone to serve. If someone isolates themselves, they won't be able to mature into a servant, for they have no one to serve. Serving a local pastor in the context of the local church enables the formation of a servant's heart.

God's highest goal for us is that we be conformed to the image of Christ (Romans 8:29). Through my years of ministering as a pastor, I've seen people who remained aloof from the local church, and I can tell you that a servant's heart was never formed in them. They may be gifted; they may be anointed; but they don't reflect the image of Christ. Therefore, they are not useful within the Body. They're no more useful for reflecting an image than wood or clay is.

We must submit ourselves *"one to another"*:

> *SUBMITTING yourselves one to another in the fear of God.* Ephesians 5:21

Jesus' image will never appear in us until we can be polished, until we have learned to *"submit ... one to another."* So if you want His image to become your own, you must find some local assembly where you can *"submit ... one to another."* That may not sound extremely spiritual, but it's the truth nevertheless. Find a local church where you can fit into the existing structure and a man to whom you can submit.

Your destiny is to reflect Christ's image. This is the will of God for your life. Therefore, you must be a vessel of silver or gold, polished in the buffer of human relationships right there in your neighborhood church. If you choose to run from this responsibility, that of fulfilling your corporate destiny in the local sense, you will be running from God's ultimate purpose for your life. If you choose to embrace your God-given responsibility, you will find life to be a joyful experience.

God is calling us to faithfulness, faithfulness to another man's vision, faithfulness to another man's responsibilities, faithfulness to the yoke of our pastors. If we are willing to do our part, He will make His image to shine forth from us. The principle of faithfulness is the foundation upon which a local body is built and upon which it functions.

What happens when God's people are faithful and take on their pastor's yoke? South Korea's Full Gospel Church of Seoul, now nearly a million members strong, is a sensational example. The people of the Yoido Full Gospel Church took on the yoke of their pastor, Dr. Paul Yonggi Cho. As they learned from him, they began to see the vision that God had given him. His vision, that of reaching the whole of Korea through cell groups, became their vision too.

When the members of Dr. Cho's church understood their pastor's vision and took his yoke upon themselves, accepting it as their own and offering their lives and homes to make it happen, they began to fulfill destiny together. They united in one goal, became one with the pastor, and as a result, the anointing from his life was imparted to them. Everywhere Korean Christians from Pastor Cho's church have gone, the same things have happened that happened under Dr. Cho's ministry in Seoul.

The entire membership of Yoido Full Gospel Church has been consecrated and set apart for a purpose by God's anointing upon Pastor Cho. Now the destiny of a nation has been changed, because God's people dared to take upon themselves their pastor's yoke. And it didn't stop in Korea. This local Korean body, fulfilling their individual and corporate destinies, has blessed the Church all over the world.

This model will work in any local church. The anointing God places upon a local leader consecrates the whole local body for a purpose. Everyone who unites with that body is consecrated for that same purpose. And great things are accomplished.

For this to happen, however, we must understand the responsibility of our leader. We must understand the purpose of his or her anointing and take his or her yoke upon ourselves. It is only when we take our leadership's yoke that we begin to fulfill destiny and share in that ministry's anointing.

"That's great!" many think, "but how can it happen when everyone is so busy living their own lives?" There is a key. It is to be found in the words of Jesus:

> *Take my yoke upon you and learn of me, for I am meek and lowly of heart.* Matthew 11:29

In these words, Jesus pointed out two characteristics about Himself:

(1) *I am meek*
(2) *[I am] lowly of heart*

It is the qualities of meekness and lowliness that allow a believer to unite himself with a local body and submit himself to their vision. It doesn't happen otherwise.

Meekness is a willingness to yield to others. Lowliness is a proper attitude toward self, not thinking more highly of one's self than one should, not possessing an overestimation of self, not feeling self-important. Lowliness means we esteem others as more important than ourselves.

This demeanor of lowliness must not be interpreted as weakness. To the contrary, it demonstrates spiritual maturity, and without it, a believer will never be a servant, will never fit into a local church structure, and will never be able to work loyally beside church leadership. May God give us the same

Spirit of meekness that was found in Jesus, and may we become willing to subordinate ourselves as He did. He said:

> *For I came down from heaven, not to do mine own will, but the will of him that sent me.*
>
> John 6:38

Jesus was meek and lowly in heart, and that's the attitude we must adopt too. When God places you in the local church, find out what the vision of that local leadership is and what their God-given responsibilities are. Then say, "Hey, I'll take your yoke on me. I'll work to do what God has commissioned you to do, pastor, as the head of this local church."

That is spiritual maturity! Seek to be delivered from the wandering spirit that is attacking Christians everywhere. Stop ambling about from church to church. Settle down under one ministry and under one man of God, and prove yourself faithful.

## Chapter Four

# The Principle of Manageability

*And when the day began to wear away, then came the twelve, and said unto him, Send the multitude away, that they may go into the towns and country round about, and lodge, and get victuals: for we are here in a desert place. But he said unto them, Give ye them to eat. And they said, We have no more but five loaves and two fishes; except we should go and buy meat for all this people. For they were about five thousand men. And he said to his disciples, Make them sit down by fifties in a company. And they did so, and made them all sit down. Then he took the five loaves and the two fishes, and looking up to heaven, he blessed them, and brake, and gave to the disciples to set before the multitude. And they did eat, and were all filled: and there was taken up of fragments that remained to them twelve baskets.* Luke 9:12-17

Jesus fed the multitudes with five loaves and two fishes. He took the bread, blessed it, broke it and gave it to His disciples to distribute to groups of fifty. Jesus took the big crowd of more than five thousand people and divided them into smaller units. In this way the task became easier to manage and oversee. Moses did this same thing, with God's blessing (Exodus 18:18-23, Deuteronomy 1:9-15).

Dividing large, unmanageable groups of people into smaller units that can be more easily managed is another principle of God's Word.

Jesus is the Head of His Body and oversees His Church throughout the world, but He also breaks it down into smaller, manageable units, which we call local churches. Some of those units are large by our standards. One example is that Full Gospel Church of Seoul, Korea. It has nearly a million members now, but in relation to the Universal Church, that is just a small unit.

Jesus, as Head of the Church, gives the oversight of local churches to an undershepherd or pastor. And each pastor whom the Lord establishes as a head in a local church has the responsibility of giving oversight to leaders of smaller units of those under his charge.

Each local church may be as large as is determined by God. The Scriptures say that He *"gives the increase."* He *"adds to the church daily such as should be saved."* He is *"the Lord of the harvest."* So only He can make that determination. He divinely breaks the universal Body of Christ into smaller units, local churches. Local churches may then be divided into even smaller units by their pastors. This allows for better oversight and facilitates ministry to individuals. This principle, biblical for sure, is wise and practical.

Just as each member of the Body is responsible before God to identify with a local assembly, each pastor is responsible before God to minister to the individuals under his care and to have the wisdom to break his larger unit into smaller, more intimate and manageable units and to place over them competent people.

Just as Jesus said to the Universal Church, *"Take my yoke upon you and learn of me,"* each local pastor must say to those under his charge, "Learn from me, and help me." He or she must get as many people as possible involved in the vision God has given for that local assembly.

It is the responsibility of the individual believer to know where God wants him to be, and he must also learn the responsibility that God has placed upon the ministers that oversee the local church to which he has been led and must identify with their particular vision, calling, and anointing, submitting to their decisions concerning how best to reach the vision.

God gives each local pastor a plan for reaching

his community. That plan is to reach *"Judea, Samaria, and the uttermost parts of the earth."* That pastor has what I call, "the vision of the house" and each member must adopt that vision as his own, putting forth every effort to bring it to pass.

When you and I, individual believers, learn the responsibilities of our pastors, our God-given leaders, and understand what their goals are, accepting them as our own, we are fulfilling our destiny in Christ.

The principle of manageability, then, is God's way of bringing order into established groups. It is His method of assuring that every believer can find his place in the local church, as well as the Universal Body of Christ. It requires that each member identify fully, not only with Jesus, the Head of the Body, but also with a leader of a local church, and that we adopt the yoke and vision of that leader as our own.

Pastors and church leaders must cry out in this present day: "TAKE MY YOKE UPON YOU." In doing so they will be saying, "I have a God-given responsibility to fulfill, but I cannot do it alone. Come and help me."

This is God's plan for His people. Embrace it.

## Chapter Five

# The Principle of Support

*And Moses said unto Joshua, Choose us out men, and go out, fight with Amalek: tomorrow I will stand on the top of the hill with the rod of God in mine hand. So Joshua did as Moses had said to him, and fought with Amalek: and Moses, Aaron, and Hur went up to the top of the hill. And it came to pass, when Moses held up his hand, that Israel prevailed: and when he let down his hand, Amalek prevailed. But Moses' hands were heavy; and they took a stone, and put it under him, and he sat thereon; and Aaron and Hur stayed up his hands, the one on the one side, and the other on the other side; and his hands were steady until the going down of the sun.*

Exodus 17:9-12

When God gives a responsibility to a leader in the Body of Christ, He also calls other people to share in that charge, just as Aaron and Hur shared the charge given to Moses. As support ministers, provided by God, they held up Moses' arms, and their selfless act allowed Israel to prevail.

Moses could not have fulfilled his responsibility as chief intercessor for Israel without support, and no minister can do what God has called him or her to do without support from other members of the Body.

Support, in this case, means more than throwing a few bills into the offering basket. Aaron and Hur remained by Moses' side, supporting him, "*until the going down of the sun.*" Their support went much further than sacrificial giving.

These two men did not second guess Moses, wondering if he had really done the right thing or why he was growing weary. They just stood faithfully by his side until victory came. Oh, may God give us some Aarons and some more Hurs today.

God called Oral Roberts to build a great seminary, but he didn't have to do it alone. God also called many people to be his partners, to share his vision, and to take that same yoke upon themselves.

God gave Kenneth Hagin the responsibility for Rhema Bible Training Center, but again He called many people to become partners with Brother Hagin in that vision. These men and women were called to take Kenneth Hagin's commission upon themselves, and they did that faithfully.

These are just two modern examples with which many of us are familiar. Every pastor who has been called by God and set by God into a certain community and given the responsibility of leading God's work in that community needs all the help he can get. God is calling us to feel our pastor's burdens, to know the "vision of the house" and to make it our own. Take the yoke upon you, and help to fulfill the vision.

This is unity! This is being one in Christ! We must function as a unit for the glory of God. Paul pled with the Corinthian believers:

> *Now I beseech you, brethren, by the name of our Lord Jesus Christ, that ye all speak the same thing, and that there be* NO DIVISIONS AMONG YOU; *but that ye be perfectly joined together in the same mind and in the same judgment.*
>
> 1 Corinthians 1:10

Those who are called by God into a local church are called to be part of the unit, to be one with their fellow brothers, to work together toward a common goal. Therefore, they must learn and practice the principle of support. When this happens, something marvelous takes place: individual Christians begin to partake of the same anointing that God has placed upon their church leaders.

The anointing flows down from the head and consecrates the whole body. The psalmist wrote:

> *Behold, how good and how pleasant it is for brethren to dwell together in UNITY! It is like the precious ointment poured on the head that ran down on the beard of Aaron [the first high priest], that came down upon the collar and skirts of his garments [consecrating the whole body]; like the dew of [lofty] Mount Hermon, and the dew that comes on the hills of Zion; for there the Lord has commanded the blessing, even life for evermore [upon the high and the lowly].*
>
> Psalm 133:1-3 (Amplified)

Every local church pastor has an anointing to reach his locale for Christ. Every ministry leader has a particular anointing to fulfill a divine purpose. It is for this reason that those who are part of the local body, who are a part of that unit, and who take their leader's yoke upon them, receive the same anointing. It flows down from the head and covers the whole body. The body, therefore, is consecrated, set apart, to fulfill the responsibility given to that leader. The head and the body, then, share the same purpose.

Many apparently feel that receiving an anointing is an easy thing to do. They imagine that the only thing they need to do is get into a prayer line and have hands laid on them and they will receive the needed impartation. The process goes much deeper than that.

"Anoint" means *to rub* or *to smear* and implies a process. Being anointed takes time. The anointing has to be rubbed and smeared on us until it is absorbed. It is not a onetime application, but rather, a continual process. We must be rubbed with God's power until it reaches the very core of our beings.

Many Christians are prayed for, yet their bondages are not broken. I believe that is because the anointing hasn't been sufficiently rubbed into their lives. They have been touched by the anointing, but it hasn't penetrated deeply enough.

To break loose from some bondages, a person must have the anointing rubbed and smeared on until it is absorbed. When that impartation comes, it is not a momentary thing. The anointing becomes a blessing that sticks with us.

God's Word declares:

> *But the anointing which ye have received of him abideth in you, and ye need not that any man teach you: but as the same anointing teacheth you of all things, and is truth, and is no lie, and even as it hath taught you, ye shall abide in him.*
>
> 1 John 2:27

The anointing is permanent. It doesn't come in a

moment's time, and it doesn't vanish in a moment's time either. In the case of the local church vision, the anointing comes by relationship, by a continual exposure to the same anointing. So God's motive for calling believers into a local church, where they are continually rubbed and smeared by the anointing, is to make them partakers of that same anointing. They get it as they lend their support to the local vision.

Another good illustration of the principle of divine support can be found in the life of young David. He was in a place called Ziklag hiding from King Saul who was in a jealous rage and seeking to kill him. While David was there in Ziklag the Scriptures say that many men of Israel came to join themselves to him:

> *Now these are they that came to David to Ziklag, while he yet kept himself close because of Saul the son of Kish: and they were among the MIGHTY MEN, HELPERS of the war.*
>
> 1 Chronicles 12:1

These *"helpers"* were sent by God to strengthen David and enable him to fulfill his God-given responsibility. Saul had displeased the Lord and David was chosen to take his place. He would be the next king of Israel, and somehow these men understood that fact:

*All these men of war, that could keep rank, CAME WITH A PERFECT HEART to Hebron, to make David king over all Israel: and all the rest also of Israel were of one heart to make David king.*

1 Chronicles 12:38

The people of Israel understood that David had been called and anointed by God for a purpose, so they were willing to take David's yoke upon themselves and help him fulfill his calling. As they did so, they were able to enjoy David's anointing and God's blessing upon the nation of Israel.

If a visiting prophet has prophesied over your pastor, just as Samuel prophesied over David, and you heard that word from God, your charge is to be like the men of war that came to David's rescue. They knew what God had revealed, and they were determined to help make it happen.

David went out to meet the men:

*If ye be come peaceably unto me to help me, mine heart shall be knit unto you: but if ye be come to betray me to mine enemies, seeing there is no wrong in mine hands, the God of our fathers look thereon, and rebuke it. Then the spirit came upon Amasai, who was chief of the captains, and he said, THINE ARE WE, David, and on thy side, thou son of Jesse: peace, peace be unto thee, and peace be to thine helpers; for thy God helpeth thee. Then*

*David received them, and made them captains of the band.* 1 Chronicles 12:17-18

David wanted to find out who among these men had an understanding of what God was doing in his life. When he found that the men understood that God had called him to be the king and that they had come to help him fulfill that vision, he gladly received them.

Today, many pastors are crying out to God for help and are searching the land desperately for those who would come and recognize the call of God upon their lives. They seek those who would recognize their God-given responsibilities, for they have need of support.

As leaders in God's armies, we need those who would say, "Hey, we're here to help you. God sent us to help you get the job done." This is God's order for His Church.

When you come to understand your leader's responsibilities, you will come to understand your own responsibilities. When you accept the responsibilities of those who are fulfilling their destiny, you will find your own destiny being developed. Don't hesitate to associate yourself in a meaningful way with a local church and a local church leadership so that your own destiny may be fulfilled.

## Chapter Six

# The Principle of Fivefold Ministry

*Therefore he saith, When he ascended up on high, he led captivity captive, and gave GIFTS unto men. ... And he gave SOME, APOSTLES; AND SOME, PROPHETS; AND SOME, EVANGELISTS; AND SOME, PASTORS AND TEACHERS; For the perfecting of the saints, for the work of the ministry, for the edifying of the body of Christ: Till we all come in the unity of the faith, and of the knowledge of the Son of God, unto a perfect man, unto the measure of the stature of the fulness of Christ: That we henceforth be no more children, tossed to and fro, and carried about with every wind of doctrine, by the sleight of men, and cunning craftiness, whereby they lie in wait to deceive; But speaking the truth in love, may grow up into him in all things, which is the head, even Christ: From whom the whole body fitly joined together and compacted by that which every joint supplieth, according to the effectual working in the measure of every part, maketh increase of the body unto the edifying of itself in love.* Ephesians 4:8,11-16

To this point we have been speaking of the local pastor, leader, or minister, but God desires to place more than just a pastor in the local assembly. He has ordained His ministry to be carried out through complementary ministry *"gifts."* This is the principle of fivefold ministry: the apostle, the prophet, the evangelist, the pastor and the teacher. I believe Peter was referring metaphorically to this group of ministers when he said:

*Humble yourselves therefore under the mighty HAND OF GOD, that he may exalt you in due time.* 1 Peter 5:6

To me, the phrase *"the mighty hand of God"* refers to God's ministry team, His representatives to the local assembly. Jesus Christ Himself is the Head of the Church, but these five *"gifts"* represent the government which He has placed over the Church upon Earth. He has delegated His authority to the fivefold ministry gifts, and the authority vested in them is demonstrated by the anointing that is upon their lives. This anointing is proof of their calling.

Recognizing the anointing that God has placed

upon His ministers and humbling ourselves under *"the mighty hand of God"* is our Christian duty as believers. We will benefit from this submission in the long run, for it is the anointed hand of the apostle, prophet, evangelist, pastor, and teacher, laid upon us, rubbing and smearing us continually, that will impart to us the same anointing.

Each of the fivefold ministry gifts have a different anointing, so that we need to be rubbed by all of them. Each one of God's fivefold ministry gifts have divinely appointed works to fulfill, and their yoke must be our yoke.

A believer needs the apostle's anointing rubbed upon his life because the apostle's anointing represents divine order. When we are exposed to the apostle's ministry, we receive an impartation of that anointing. When it has been imparted, it works in us, and the characteristics of an apostolic anointing begin to be visible in our lives as well. An impartation of the apostle's gift will bring divine order to us. Biblical structure will be evidenced, and we'll be set in order with biblical priorities. We'll understand authority and accountability, because these are the primary messages of the apostle's foundational ministry.

When the Apostle Paul wrote to the Colossian church, he said:

> *For though I be absent in the flesh, yet am I with*

*you in the spirit, joying and beholding YOUR ORDER, and the stedfastness of your faith in Christ.* Colossians 2:5

When an apostle views a local church, or even an individual Christian's life, the revelation God gives is of order, or the lack of it, within that church's or that Christian's life. And through the ministry of the apostle, rubbing and smearing on the apostle's doctrine and anointing, the church or individual will be set in order.

The Apostle Paul felt compelled to deal with abuses in the Lord's Supper in Corinth. After he had given the Corinthians lengthy instructions on how to straighten out their confusion, he told them:

*And if any man hunger, let him eat at home; that ye come not together unto condemnation. And the rest will I SET IN ORDER when I come.*
1 Corinthians 11:34

An apostle has the duty of setting doctrinal, spiritual and church affairs in order. This ministry is significant for a Christian's walk with God.

A prophet's ministry brings the anointing of revelation.

When we sit under the prophet's ministry, the spirit of wisdom and revelation flows into us. We learn to hear the voice of the Lord. His voice becomes real to us. This happens when the prophet is able to rub and smear his anointing into us.

Even King Saul benefited from exposure to the prophetic gift. He learned to hear from God and prophesy:

> *After that thou shalt come to the hill of God, where is the garrison of the Philistines: and it shall come to pass, when thou art come thither to the city, that thou shalt meet a company of prophets coming down from the high place with a psaltery, and a tabret, and a pipe, and a harp, before them; and they shall prophesy: And the Spirit of the LORD will come upon thee, and THOU SHALT PROPHESY with them, and SHALT BE TURNED INTO ANOTHER MAN. And let it be, when these signs are come unto thee, that thou do as occasion serve thee; for God is with thee.* 1 Samuel 10:5-7

We also need the ministry of evangelist, because the evangelist's is a ministry of power and demonstration of the Holy Ghost. The evangelist imparts inspiration to our lives. The apostle brings ordination, the prophet brings revelation, but the evangelist brings inspiration and exhortation.

Philip is a case in point:

> *Therefore they that were scattered abroad went every where preaching the word. Then Philip went down to the city of Samaria, and preached Christ*

*unto them. And the people with one accord gave heed unto those things which Philip spake,* HEARING AND SEEING THE MIRACLES WHICH HE DID. *For unclean spirits, crying with loud voice, came out of many that were possessed with them: and many taken with palsies, and that were lame, were healed. And there was great joy in that city.*

Acts 8:4-8

An evangelist's anointing brings the consuming zeal of God to the believer. The Holy Ghost's fire is imparted to him, and he is consumed in doing what God has purposed in his life.

Miracles, signs and wonders are also elements of the evangelist's anointing.

The anointing of the pastor is a vital ingredient in a believer's walk because the pastor's anointing is to affirm. A pastor lives with his sheep and is able to continually affirm them in their faith. Through the pastor's anointing, the members of the flock learn how to love one another and even, how to affirm one another.

Jesus was concerned as he looked at the multitudes roaming about Jerusalem without a shepherd:

*When he saw the crowds, he had compassion on them, because they were harassed and helpless, like sheep* WITHOUT A SHEPHERD.

Matthew 9:36

Jesus knew that people need a pastor. Every one of us must allow ourselves to be fitted into a local church. This will make us loving people, as the pastor's anointing is smeared and rubbed on us until bitterness, resentment, and unforgiveness are gone, and the love of Christ envelops us. Thus, we are affirmed by the pastor's ministry.

The teaching gift's anointing is for providing information. When a Christian is exposed to a minister who has God's call to teach, his faith is perfected. Paul, the Apostle, writing to the Thessalonians, said:

> *Night and day praying exceedingly that we might see your face, and might perfect that which is lacking in your faith.* 1 Thessalonians 3:10

Paul was concerned about the Thessalonians. A lack of knowledge results in a lack of faith. So he intended to perfect that which was lacking in their faith by teaching them and filling up their lack of knowledge.

Paul wrote to the Colossians:

> *To whom God would make known what is the riches of the glory of this mystery among the Gentiles; which is Christ in you, the hope of glory: Whom we preach, warning every man, and* TEACHING EVERY MAN *in all wisdom; that we may present every man perfect in Christ Je-*

*sus: Whereunto I also labour, striving according to his working, which worketh in me mightily.*
Colossians 1:27-29

Preaching is warning or announcing the facts of the Gospel, but teaching is explaining the facts of the Gospel. Through both preaching and teaching, God's saints are perfected, brought to completion in Christ.

An apostle's ministry is ordination, the prophet's is revelation, an evangelist's is inspiration, a pastor's is affirmation and the teacher's is information.

Christ's Universal Body desperately needs the fivefold ministry gifting operating locally and in each Christian's individual life, bringing each one to completion and perfection. We need more than an occasional touch. We need a continual rubbing of these anointings into each Christian's life, rubbing until there is an impartation, a transference, from each of the fivefold ministry gifts into the life of every individual believer.

The psalmist wrote:

*I shall be anointed with fresh oil.* Psalm 92:10

When the anointing is imparted, then the characteristic of each anointing — order, revelation, love, power, and faith — will become part of us. Jesus said to His disciples:

## The Principle of Fivefold Ministry

*He that receiveth you receiveth me, and he that receiveth me receiveth him that sent me.*

Matthew 10:40

Jesus told those to whom He ministered that if they would receive a prophet in the name of a prophet, they would receive a prophet's reward. He was saying that if we are willing to recognize and identify a ministry gift, such as prophet, and receive that prophet's ministry into our lives, we will receive a reward from the prophet — his grace or anointing.

This is true of today's believers and today's prophets as well. The operation of the Spirit that is within a ministry gift, when shared with us, brings impartation to us, as we recognize and accept that ministry gift.

## Chapter Seven

# Removing the Excuses

*The Spirit of the Lord is upon me, because he hath anointed me to preach the gospel to the poor; he hath sent me to heal the brokenhearted, to preach deliverance to the captives, and recovering of sight to the blind, to set at liberty them that are bruised.* Luke 4:18

Many people have been hurt and wounded in local church situations. I have personally observed many such incidents. Over the past fifteen years that I have been a pastor, I have had to deal with Christians who have been abused, misused, and discouraged. It's sad, and my heart goes out to them, but if every Christian that has been hurt in church relationships were to stop coming to church, Sunday services could not be held any more; for we have all been hurt at some time, lay people and ministers alike.

Because Christians are overcomers, and they can overcome their hurts and become willing to forgive and to trust again, churches are filled these days. Thank God for His grace.

But being hurt is just one of the things that causes Christians to be reluctant to become involved in a local church. I have identified at least four such things:

The more common thing that causes people to be unwilling to become involved in a local church situation is an elitist attitude. They feel so spiritual that they don't think they need the same spiritual care that everyone else needs. If this were true, God would have exempted certain ones, but it isn't so. We all need the fivefold ministry gifts in our lives, including the operation of the gift of pastor.

Having been hurt may rank second, and many people are reluctant to get involved in a local church because someone has hurt them in the past. Because we have a Savior that is a healer of broken hearts, however, and Who is ready to heal all the hurting, how can we stay hurt? Jesus said:

> *The Spirit of the Lord is upon me, because he hath anointed me to preach the gospel to the poor; he hath sent me to heal the brokenhearted, to preach deliverance to the captives, and recovering of sight to the blind, TO SET AT LIBERTY THEM THAT ARE BRUISED.* Luke 4:18

Let Him heal all your bruises and wounds and make you whole again so that you can get involved in what He is doing in these last days.

A third thing that makes some people reluctant to become involved in a local church is a feeling of inferiority. These persons may have low self-esteem. They may feel worthless as a result of negative words and experiences they have encountered in life. They may be so self-conscious that they feel everyone else views them in an unfavorable way. Consequently, they cannot face people.

There is a cure for a poor self-image and an inferiority complex. It is renewing one's mind with the Word of God. If we read His Word long enough, we will eventually start seeing ourselves as He sees us. Our estimation of our own self-worth must be based upon the value that God Himself has placed on our lives. After all, we have *"put on the new man"*:

> *And that ye PUT ON THE NEW MAN, which after God is created in righteousness and true holiness.* Ephesians 4:24

If we can renew our minds, we will be delivered from the feeling of inferiority and low self-esteem that plague many.

A fourth reason that many are unwilling to get involved in the local church is an unwillingness to change. This is often the result of stubbornness of heart and rebellion. God shows this to be a terrible sin, as serious as witchcraft:

> *For rebellion is as the sin of witchcraft, and stubbornness is as iniquity and idolatry.*
>
> 1 Samuel 15:23

Witchcraft seeks to control, and someone who has a spirit of witchcraft attempts to maintain dominance and control over the lives of others. Likewise, stubbornness shows its ugly head when we insist on keeping control over our own lives. Both these types of control are equally abominable in God's eyes. So people who refuse to change are in danger of losing their very soul. We must embrace change at every turn.

These are the four most common reasons I have encountered that keep people from getting involved in the local church, and those who use these excuses suffer. When any person, however, refuses to use such excuses and gets involved with the local church, begins to learn the vision of local leadership, and through lowliness and meekness of heart, takes the local yoke upon themselves, that person is going to be blessed. Healing and restoration will come to their lives as they follow God's principles. By taking their leader's yoke upon themselves, they being to fulfill their own divine destiny.

Maybe I could ask you personally: Do you know what the responsibility of your pastor is in God's overall program? Do you understand your pastor's vision? Have you come to the place where you have said, "I'll take that yoke. I am willing to work toward the fulfillment of the responsibilities God has given my leadership"? It takes real meekness and lowliness to do that, but the results are wonderful. Jesus said, *"You shall find rest for your souls."* What a beautiful truth!

> *Take my yoke upon you, and learn of me; for I am meek and lowly in heart: and ye shall find rest unto your souls.* Matthew 11:29 (NIV)

Every struggle is over when you accept the Lord's yoke. *You shall find rest.*

People don't burn out because they've done too much work for the Lord, but because they have struggled and wrestled with God for too long. They have been at war with themselves. They have been unwilling to obey God and have been fighting not to yield to His plan for their destiny. They are weary, not from too much work, but from fighting with God.

Jesus taught us that if we become *meek and lowly in heart,* if we are willing to take our leader's *yoke* upon us, we can find rest for our souls. This word translated *rest* may also be translated as *recreation.* It means: *refreshment of the strength and spirits after toil.* Praise God for that!

Do you want to have spiritual recreation and a

refreshing of your strength and spirit? If so, through lowliness and meekness of heart, take your leader's yoke upon yourself. Amen!

This is a great promise, and everyone should receive it.

You don't have to be burned out. You don't have to war within yourself and struggle continually. You can rest in the Lord merely by taking His yoke upon you, both His yoke to fulfill The Great Commission and His yoke to fulfill God-given responsibility locally with your church leadership.

The Apostle Paul understood this principle of being yoked together with people and took it to mean sharing a God-given responsibility:

> *Therefore, my brethren dearly beloved and longed for, my joy and crown, so stand fast in the Lord, my dearly beloved. I beseech Euodias, and beseech Syntyche, that they be of the same mind in the Lord. And I intreat thee also, TRUE YOKEFELLOW, help those women which laboured with me in the gospel, with Clement also, and with other my fellowlabourers, whose names are in the book of life. Rejoice in the Lord alway: and again I say, Rejoice.* Philippians 4:1-4

Paul was speaking to a *"yokefellow,"* a person who had taken the Apostle's yoke upon himself.

Paul had an itinerant ministry of worldwide proportions. He was a church planter, and God called people to help him with his responsibilities. We may think of these people as Paul's apostolic team. We can read about them in the Word.

In Romans 16:1-12, Paul gave a list of people who were part of his apostolic team — his yokefellows.

Writing to Timothy, Paul said:

> *Whereunto I am appointed a preacher, and an apostle, and a teacher of the Gentiles.*
>
> 2 Timothy 1:11

Paul knew his responsibilities, and his co-laborers knew them too. They understood his yoke of responsibility and had made a conscious decision to be yokefellows with him, partners together with him, to accomplish God-given responsibilities. By so doing, they were fulfilling both their individual and their corporate destinies.

The Apostle Paul and his fellow laborers experienced great fulfillment. They understood destiny. They were meek and low of heart. They shared and worked together. They strived to fulfill a common goal of God-given duty that had been given to Paul — an apostolic responsibility.

So every Christian needs to learn from those over them in the Lord, finding out what their God-given responsibilities are. Then they should take that yoke upon themselves. If they are willing to do this, they will be fulfilling destiny by fulfilling God-given responsibility, and they won't have to wait for some future responsibility that has been promised them by prophecy.

When we begin to understand the responsibilities that have been given to another and take that responsibility upon ourselves, God will give us our own responsibility (see Luke 16:12). After we have shown ourselves faithful with another man's affairs, God will give us a ministry of our own.

Many believers have received prophecies that they would be given some great ministry. These prophecies are true and valid. Perhaps the prophetic word has declared a ministry of apostle, or prophet, or pastor, and the recipient is wanting to take on that responsibility to fulfill destiny. But he cannot fulfill that destiny until he first submits to scriptural principles and helps another man or woman of God fulfill their destiny. No man can achieve his own destiny until he has taken his leader's yoke and been proven faithful to it. There is no substitute for faithfulness.

Once we submit to God's principles, the prophecies that we have received will come to pass. God will give us our own responsibility and bring others to help fulfill it.

So, if you've been hurt, hope is still knocking at the door of your destiny. Lift your eyes from self, focus them on Jesus, get the vision, and then get busy with His yoke. It will bring you rest.

# Part IV:

# *The Third Dimension of Your Destiny*

CHAPTER EIGHT

# INDIVIDUAL DESTINY

*For as we have many members in one body, and ALL MEMBERS HAVE NOT THE SAME OFFICE: So we, being many, are one body in Christ, and every one members one of another. Having then gifts differing according to the grace that is given to us, whether prophecy, let us prophesy according to the proportion of faith; Or ministry, let us wait on our ministering: or he that teacheth, on teaching; Or he that exhorteth, on exhortation: he that giveth, let him do it with simplicity; he that ruleth, with diligence; he that sheweth mercy, with cheerfulness.*

Romans 12:4-8

Thus far, we have learned that there are two levels of destiny: (1) corporate destiny in the universal sense, which relates us to the whole Body of Christ and (2) corporate destiny in the local sense, which relates us to the local church where God has placed us.

We have learned that taking the yoke of leadership upon ourselves is to learn our leader's God-given responsibilities and then let them become our very own, as we work to fulfill them. In order to do so, Jesus taught that we would need to be lowly and meek of heart and we would need to be a part of a team, taking the servant's place within our local church. The result, which Jesus taught was desirable, would be rest for our souls. There would be an end of our struggles. The warring within to keep control of our own destiny would be over. In the process, we would be spiritually refreshed and invigorated. Now we want to look carefully at individual destiny.

Individual destiny is individual responsibility, and God gives it to you based upon your God-given abilities. Peter wrote to the church:

> *As every man hath received the gift, even so minister the same one to another, as good stewards of the manifold grace of God.* 1 Peter 4:10

Each of us has different gifts:

> *For as we have many members in one body, and ALL MEMBERS HAVE NOT THE SAME OFFICE: So we, being many, are one body in Christ, and every one members one of another. Having then gifts differing according to the grace that is*

*given to us, whether prophecy, let us prophesy according to the proportion of faith; Or ministry, let us wait on our ministering: or he that teacheth, on teaching; Or he that exhorteth, on exhortation: he that giveth, let him do it with simplicity; he that ruleth, with diligence; he that sheweth mercy, with cheerfulness.* Romans 12:4-8

This seems to be very clear. God has placed a variety of gifts in the Body of Christ. Our responsibilities, therefore, are related to the gifts we have been given. For example, if you have a God-given ability to sing, you should respond to that ability. You should take responsibility for that gifting in your life. Taking responsibility simply means to respond to His ability within you. You will fulfill your personal destiny as you use your God-given abilities. And this can be done in the context of our local church as well as on the job and at home.

First, we must get the big picture, the vision of the house, the responsibility that God has given that church's leader. Then find out how you can use your own individual abilities to fulfill that vision, which will require the use of all the various gifts and abilities that God has given the people in that local church.

Even when Jesus was here on Earth, those who followed Him had very different gifts and abilities, and very different personalities. Together, they comprised a team that helped Jesus fulfill His mission.

Those who made up Paul's team had very different gifts. By chosing to yoke themselves to him, they joined those gifts in a common cause. Barnabus was an encourager. Apollos was mighty in the Word of God. Aquilla and Priscilla were in-depth teachers. Others in Paul's company had gifts of giving. Together, they made up a powerful team and by fulfilling a corporate destiny, they fulfilled their personal destiny. They used their God-given abilities to work towards the apostle's larger vision.

This is Biblical order. This is New Testament ministry. This is the way the Holy Spirit works in the Church today.

Jesus, in the parable of the talents, said:

> *For the kingdom of heaven is as a man travelling into a far country, who called his own servants, and delivered unto them his goods. And unto one he gave five talents, to another two, and to another one; to every man ACCORDING TO HIS SEVERAL ABILITY; and straightway took his journey.* Matthew 25:14-15

The Lord gives people responsibility based upon the grace that is available to their lives. He will never give us a responsibility for which He has not provided us sufficient grace.

If you have an ability to relate to children and speak the Word of God to them in a way that they can grasp and assimilate, then it is likely that your individual destiny will be to work with children. If you have an ability to care for and comfort the elderly, your individual destiny will probably be in relationship to that particular age group within the church. If you have an ability for taking care of details, your destiny may be fulfilled working in the administration of the church. God will give us responsibility based on the gifts that He has placed in our life. When we use that ability, we fulfill our individual destiny.

> *So then every one of us shall give account of himself to God.* Romans 14:12

Each of us will give account to the Lord. We will be held responsible for the grace He has placed in our lives and how we have used it to fulfill His divine purposes. We are told:

> *Obey them that have the rule over you, and submit yourselves: for they watch for your souls, as they that must give account, that they may do it with joy, and not with grief: for that is unprofitable for you.* Hebrews 13:17

Local church leadership has the responsibility of offering guidance to individual Christians within the church. This does not include control over them, coercing or dictating to them, but rather, it is giving guidance and lovingly suggesting the best possible place of service for them within the house.

Pastors can be very helpful to individual Christians who are seeking to fulfill destiny within the local church. They do this by recognizing their charge's God-given abilities and guiding him or her to opportunities in which their individual ability will be useful. When a pastor recognizes our abilities and affirms them, confidence rises up within us to step out and use our God-given gift.

There are also times when leadership must call people into account for the use, or the lack of use, of their spiritual gifts. Paul called Timothy into account for a lack of use of his God-given gifts:

> *NEGLECT NOT THE GIFT that is in thee, which was given thee by prophecy, with the laying on of the hands of the presbytery.* 1 Timothy 4:14

Timothy was pastoring the church in Ephesus and was encountering some difficulties in the fulfillment of his responsibilities there. He had become fearful. Paul, as Timothy's pastor, wrote to him and encouraged him, telling him to stir up his God-given gifts and use them. Paul knew that if Timothy would use his God-given abilities, he would find success in his life and be able to fulfill divine purpose.

This is also true of us, as individual Christians. I would encourage you to allow local church leadership to stir you. Use what God has given you, even though sometimes you may be reluctant or fearful. Getting involved isn't always easy, but it is the best path.

It is paradoxical, but there are some Christians who are obviously gifted by God in some area, but they run from it. Perhaps, in the exercise of their talent, something happened that hurt them and fear entered. But don't keep that gift hidden. Stir it up. Fulfill your destiny.

Remember, there are people within the local church who will love you and affirm you. They will encourage you. Just learn to use what God has given you. You will be spiritually refreshed and your soul will be given divine recreation.

You have a God-given destiny and a place in the overall purposes of God for His church in these last days. I encourage you to discover, develop and deploy your spiritual gifting within the house where the Lord has set you. I encourage you to learn the vision of the house, learn the responsibility of your pastor and take that yoke upon you in lowliness and meekness of heart.

Take the yoke of Jesus, the Great Shepherd and Head of the Church Universal, and become a Great-Commission Christian. You'll be fulfilling your corporate and your individual destiny. Be a part of the last day's revival that God is bringing upon the Earth — just as He promised.

# Notes